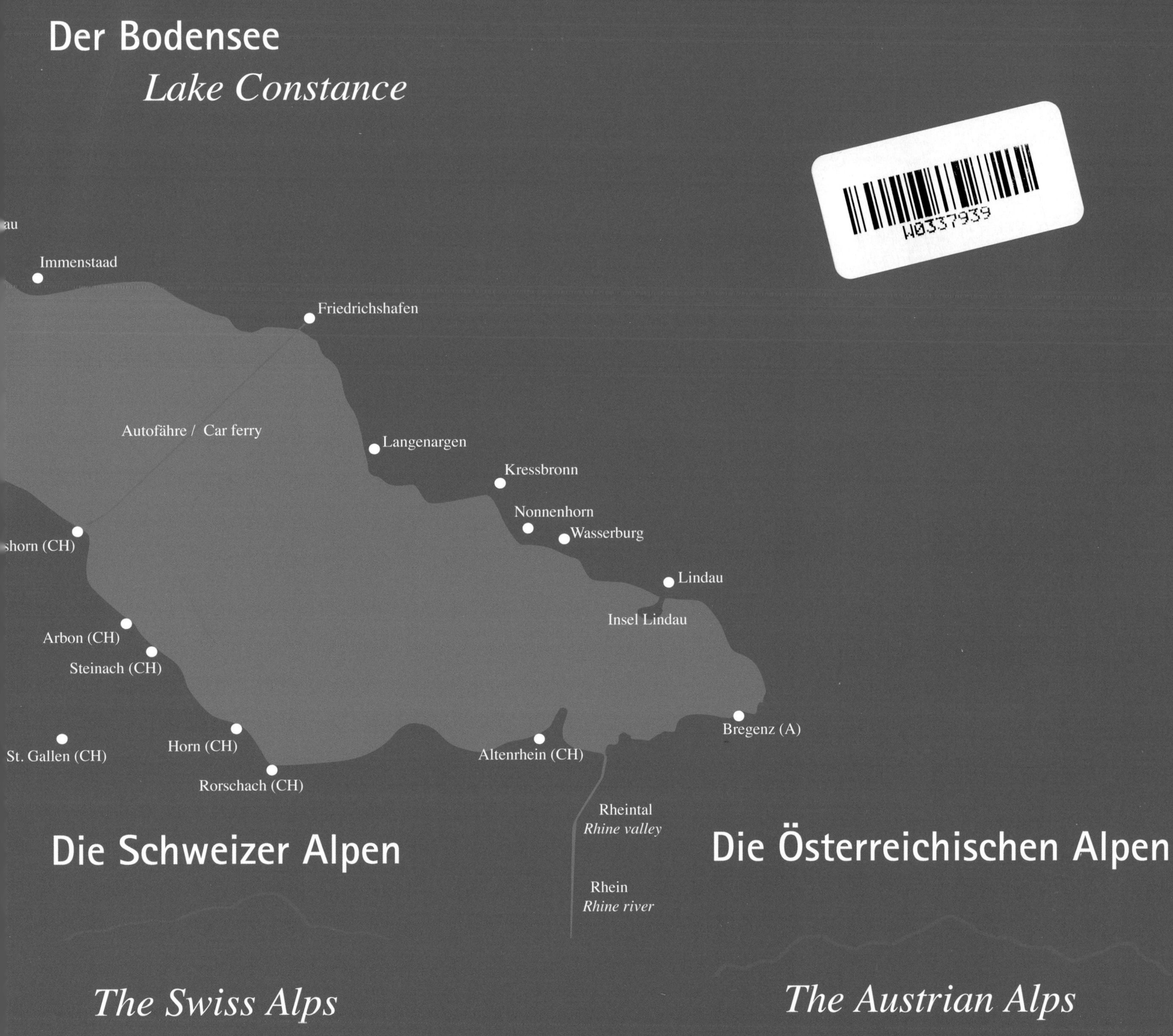
Der Bodensee
Lake Constance
au
Immenstaad
Friedrichshafen
Autofähre / Car ferry
Langenargen
Kressbronn
Nonnenhorn
Wasserburg
Lindau
Insel Lindau
shorn (CH)
Arbon (CH)
Steinach (CH)
St. Gallen (CH)
Horn (CH)
Rorschach (CH)
Altenrhein (CH)
Bregenz (A)
Rheintal
Rhine valley
Rhein
Rhine river
Die Schweizer Alpen
The Swiss Alps
Die Österreichischen Alpen
The Austrian Alps

Bodenseeflug

Flight over Lake Constance

Eine Bilderreise über den Bodensee

A Pictorial Journey over Lake Constance

Photos Stanko Petek

VerlagPetek

Stanko Petek begann mit seiner Fliegerlaufbahn im Jahre 1977. Als einer der ersten Piloten folgte er dem Reiz der noch jungen Sportart Drachenfliegen. Seine Ausbildung zum Drachenfluglehrer ermöglichte ihm 1981 den Sprung in die Selbstständigkeit. 1983 war er wieder bei den Pionieren der neuen Luftsportart Ultraleichtfliegen, zunächst auf den so genannten „Trikes". Diese Luftsportart wurde seinerzeit im Volksmund noch etwas spöttisch „Rasenmäherfliegen" genannt. Auch hier folgte unmittelbar die Ausbildung zum Fluglehrer. Fortschrittliche Technik und der Einsatz bester HighTech-Materialien ließen die Ultraleichtflugzeuge im Lauf der Jahre zu den leisesten, innovativsten und ökologisch-ökonomischsten Luftfahrzeugen werden, weshalb Stanko Petek seine Fluglehrertätigkeit 1992 komplett in diese Sparte verlegte. Folgerichtig war als nächster Schritt die Ausbildung zum Privatflugzeugführer im Jahr 1994 und der Umstieg auf die so genannten „dreiachsgesteuerten" Sportflugzeuge. Im selben Jahr folgte sein autodidaktischer Einstieg in die Luftbildfotografie. Es entwickelte sich eine grenzenlose Leidenschaft, stets gepaart mit dem Anspruch an höchstmögliche Qualität. Aus diesem Grund fotografiert Stanko Petek mit einer Hasselblad H3D II oder auf Wunsch mit einer speziellen Luftbildkamera der Marke Linhof Aerotechnika im Dia-Großformat 4x5 inch (10x12cm). Schnell wurden seine Bilder - insbesondere die herrlichen Landschaftsaufnahmen des Bodensees – zur „Luftbildkunst". Seit Jahren bereichern diese schönen Aufnahmen diverse Kalender, Bücher und Bildbände. Im Jahr 2003 erfolgte die Gründung eines eigenen Verlages. Die gleichbleibende Qualität seiner Arbeit sichert Stanko Petek einen zufriedenen Kundenstamm aus Marketing und Industrie. Die fotografischen Auftragsarbeiten führt er mittlerweile quer durch Europa aus. Weitere „Bilderreisen" ermöglicht Ihnen das Internetportal www.LUFTBILD.com.

Stanko Petek began his flying career in 1977. He was one of the first pilots to be involved in the exciting new sport of hang gliding. Having completed his hang gliding instructor's course, he decided to become self-employed in 1981. By 1983 he pioneering ardour had got him involved in yet another new kind of sport flying microlight planes, beginning with „Trikes". In the early days, this new sport was often referred to rather unkindly as „lawn-mower flying". Stanko Petek decided to take an instructor's course for this sport too. Modern engineering and the use of high-tech materials has enabled microlight planes to become the most quiet, innovative, efficient and environmentally-friendly aircraft in the skies. Indeed, because of these developments, Stanko Petek decided to concentrate solely on microlighting instruction in 1992. The next logical step in his career was to take his private aircraft pilot's licence in 1994 and make the switch to „three-axis controlled" planes. The beginning of his self-taught career in aerial photography began in the same year. This career decision was to develop into a real passion for photography and a driving desire to achieve the very best quality. To this end, Stanko Petek takes all his pictures with a Hasselblad H3D II or a specially-developed aerial picture camera by Linhof Aerotechnika which takes large-size 4 x 5 inch (10x12cm) slides. His pictures soon became regarded as „aerial art", especially his breathtaking scenic shots of Lake Constance. These beautiful pictures have been used to adorn a large number of calendars, books and illustrated books for many years. Stanko Petek founded his own publishing company in 2003. The reliable quality of Stanko Peteks photographic work has enabled him to establish a secure customer base from industry and the marketing sector. He now carries out photographic commissions for customers right across Europe. You can enjoy more of his „photographic journeys" by visiting www.LUFTBILD.com.

Radolfzell mit Blick über die Kernstadt mit dem dominanten Münster und der Halbinsel Mettnau.
Radolfzell with view over the streches across the inner city and the *Mettnau* peninsula.

Radolfzell am Bodensee, die Heimatstadt des Luftbildfotografen Stanko Petek.
Radolfzell at *Lake Constance*, the hometown of the aerial photographer *Stanko Petek*.

Diese Perspektive zeigt deutlich die Abgrenzung des Altstadtkerns von Radolfzell am Bodensee. Das Zentrum bildet das Münster mit dem Marktplatz.

This perspective clearly shows how the old town area of *Radolfzell, Lake Constance*, is separated from the rest of the town. The cathedral with its marketplace forms the centre of the town.

Neben der Halbinsel Mettnau liegt die Liebesinsel, die kleinste Insel im Bodensee, welche den Namen nicht zuletzt ihrer romantischen und idyllischen Lage mitten im Naturschutzgebiet zu verdanken hat.
In the middle of the nature reserve and besides the *Mettnau* peninsula is the *Liebesinsel* (Island of Love) which is one of the smallest, but not at least one of the most beautiful islands at the *Lake Constance*.

Paradiesische Idylle am westlichen Bodensee: Der Untersee mit Radolfzell, der Insel Reichenau, der Halbinsel Höri und mit einem fantastischen Panorama zu den schneebedeckten Alpen.

Paradise-like scene on the western shores of *Lake Constance*: The *Untersee* (lower lake) with *Radolfzell*, the Island of *Reichenau*, the *Höri* peninsula and wonderfully panoramic views across to the snow-covered alps.

Die Ortschaft Markelfingen stand Pate bei der Namensgebung der dazugehörigen Bucht, dem Markelfinger Winkel.
The community of *Markelfingen* lent its name to the nearby bay the *Markelfinger Winkel*.

Die Ortschaft Allensbach liegt am sogenannten Gnadensee. Die Legende sagt: Wurde im Mittelalter ein Delinquent mit dem Boot vom Gerichtsort auf der Insel Reichenau zum Galgenberg auf dem Festland transportiert und es erklang während der Überfahrt eine Kirchenglocke, so wurde er begnadigt.
The community of *Allensbach* is located at the *Gnadensee* (lake of pardon). The legend tells us that in the Middle Ages if a church bell rang out while a criminal was being transported by boat from the court island of *Reichenau* to *Galgenberg* (hill of gallows) on the Mainland, he would receive pardon.

Das Kloster Hegne: Konstanzer Bischöfe nutzten Hegne als Sommerresidenz. Seit 1892 befindet sich das herrschaftliche Anwesen im Besitz des Ordens Barmherzige Schwestern vom Heiligen Kreuz.

The *Hegne* Convent: *Hegne* serves as a summer residence for bishops from *Constance*. This stately estate has belonged to the *Barmherzige Schwestern vom Heiligen Kreuz* order since 1892.

Die Insel Reichenau nach dem Durchzug einer Kaltfront und bei „Rückseiten-Wetterlage". Viele Surfer genießen einen Traumtag bei fünf Windstärken.

The island of *Reichenau* in the wake of a cold front and strong winds. A large number of surfers enjoying a wonderful day and wind force five.

Die Insel Reichenau wurde im Jahre 2000 von der UNESCO zum Weltkulturerbe ernannt.
The island of *Reichenau*, since the year 2000 a World *UNESCO* Cultural Heritage site.

Winteridylle am Westufer der Reichenau mit der Kirche St. Peter & Paul, Niederzell.
An idyllic winter scene on the western shores of *Reichenau* island with the church of *St. Peter & Paul, Niederzell.*

Nach seinem Durchfluss durch den Obersee mündet der Rhein am sogenannten „Rheintrichter" und fließt als „Seerhein" in den Untersee. Konstanz wird über drei Brücken verbunden, im Bild hinten die „Neue Rheinbrücke", vorn erkennt man die „Alte Rheinbrücke".
After flowing through the *Obersee* (upper lake), the *Rhine* flows into the so-called *Rheintrichter* and on into the *Untersee* (lower lake) as the *Seerhein*. *Constance* is linked by three bridges; at the back of the picture the *New Rhine* bridge while in the front you can see the *Old Rhine* bridge.

Die Altstadt von Konstanz mit dem Konstanzer Münster (ehemalige Kathedralkirche des Bistums).
View over the historic town of *Constance* with its cathedral (the former cathedral of the diocese *Constance*).

Ein Abstecher über Kreuzlingen (Schweiz) bietet uns einen Blick über die Konstanzer Altstadt und zum „Seerhein".
Taking a detour over *Kreuzlingen (Switzerland)* opens up views across to the old town area of *Constance* and to the so called *„Seerhein"*.

Im Abendrot der untergehenden Sonne passieren wir die Insel Mainau, einen touristischen Magnet am Bodensee. Besondere Attraktionen sind das Palmen- und das Schmetterlingshaus. Diese Aufnahme entstand an der Sommersonnwende.

While afterglowing of the sunset, we pass the island of *Mainau* with its famous attractions of the Palm Tree and Butterfly houses. This picture was taken on the summer solstice.

Das Schloß auf der Insel Mainau wird umringt von fantastischen Blumenbeeten, dem wunderschönen Rosengarten und einer Vielzahl tropischer Pflanzen, welche man insbesondere im Palmenhaus bewundern kann.

The castle on the island of *Mainau* is encircled by wonderful flowerbeds, the beautiful Rose garden and a large number of tropical plants, some are located in the famous Palm house.

Blick über Wallhausen und Dingelsdorf zur Insel Mainau mit Bodenseepanorama.
Views over *Wallhausen, Dingelsdorf, Mainau* and the *Lake Constance* panorama in the background.

Bodman am Überlinger See, Wohnsitz des Künstlers Peter Lenk.
Bodman, Überlinger See, hometown of the artist *Peter Lenk.*

Blick über die Ortschaft Ludwigshafen am westlichen Ende des Überlinger Sees.
Views over *Ludwigshafen* on the far western shores of the *Überlinger See.*

Blick über die Ortschaft Sipplingen, die ihre Bekanntheit erlangt als Entnahmestelle von Bodenseewasser zur Trinkwasserversorgung.
Views of the community of *Sipplingen*, which is well-known for being the point where the water of *Lake Constance* is converted into drinking water.

Überlingen am Bodensee. Im Vordergrund erkennen wir die Bodensee-Therme, welche sich bereits nach kurzer Zeit großer Beliebtheit als Stätte der Erholung erfreut.

Überlingen at *Lake Constance*. In the foreground we can see the *„Bodensee-Therme"* (wellness and swimming complex), which soon became very popular as a place of leisure and relaxation.

Der Altstadtkern der freien Reichstadt Überlingen am Bodensee.
Überlingen, Lake Constance, centre of the historic town in this free imperial city.

Aus Nordwesten bietet sich uns ein atemberaubender Blick über die Stadt Überlingen zur Insel Mainau und zu den Schweizer Alpen.
From the northwest we are treated to breathtaking views across the town of *Überlingen* to the island of *Mainau* and the *Swiss alps*.

Beliebtes Ausflugsziel am Bodensee: Die Klosterkirche Birnau, eingebettet in herrliche Weinberge.
One of *Lake Constance's* favourite beauty spots is the monastery church of *Birnau*, nestled among beautiful vineyards.

Die Bodenseegemeinde Uhldingen-Mühlhofen ist weit über die Grenzen berühmt für ihre Pfahlbauten. Ein Luftschiff fliegt auf seiner westlichen Route zurück nach Friedrichshafen.

The community of *Uhldingen-Mühlhofen* at *Lake Constance* has achieved international fame for its lake dwellings. An airship is returning back from a westward route to *Friedrichshafen*.

Sonnenuntergang über den Pfahlbauten der Gemeinde Unteruhldingen.
Sunset over the lake dwellings of the community *Unteruhldingen.*

Wo die Steinzeit zu neuem Leben erweckt wurde: Das berühmte Pfahlbaumuseum in Unteruhldingen.
Bringing the Stone Age back to life: The famous *lake dwelling museum* in *Unteruhldingen.*

Das Pfahlbaumuseum in Unteruhldingen mit Panoramablick zum Säntis.
The *lake dwelling museum* in *Unteruhldingen* with panoramic view to mount *Säntis.*

Die Stadt Meersburg am nördlichen Bodenseeufer: Touristischer Magnet und bestens bekannt für die Herstellung erlesener Bodenseeweine.

The town of *Meersburg* on the northern shores of *Lake Constance* is a magnet for tourists and well-known for the production of fine *Lake Constance* wines.

In der Meersburg, auch „Altes Schloss" genannt, lebte in den Jahren 1841 bis 1848 die berühmte deutsche Dichterin Annette von Droste-Hülshoff, wo sie auch am 24. Mai 1848 verstarb. Ihre Wohnräume und das Sterbezimmer sind Teil des Rundgangs.
The famous German poetess *Annette von Droste-Hülshoff* lived in the *Meersburg*, also known as the „Old Castle", from 1841 until her death on the 24th of May 1848. Her living quarters and the room in which she died are part of the tour.

Die Weinbaugemeinde Hagnau am Bodensee, eingerahmt von zahlreichen Obstbaumplantagen und Weinbergen.
The winegrowing community of *Hagnau, Lake Constance* with its numerous fruit-growing plantations and vineyards.

Immenstaad - das HighTech-Zentrum der Luft und Raumfahrt am Bodensee.
Immenstaad - the high-tech aerospace industry centre with a view over *Lake Constance.*

Die Schlosskirche in Friedrichshafen mit den beiden 55 Meter hohen Kuppeltürmen ist das Wahrzeichen der Stadt. Sie zählt zu den berühmtesten oberschwäbischen Bauwerken des Barock.

The castle-church in *Friedrichshafen* with its two 55-metre-tall domed towers forms the town's landmark. The church is one of the most famous baroque buildings in the upper Swabian region.

Friedrichshafen ist das Industriezentrum des nördlichen Bodensees. Auf diesem Bild zeigt uns die Stadt ihre schönste Seite mit der Uferpromenade und der Hafenanlage.

Friedrichshafen is the industrial center of the northern *Lake Constance* region. Here the town is pictured from its most beautiful side with its esplanade and harbour area.

Up, up and away... vom Bodensee-Airport Friedrichshafen in die schönsten Urlaubsgebiete Europas.
Up, up and away... from *Bodensee-Airport Friedrichshafen, Lake Constance* to some of Europe's most attractive holiday destinations.

Der Bodensee-Airport Friedrichshafen mit seiner Start- und Landebahn, rechts im Bild die „Neue Messe" Friedrichshafen.
The *Bodensee-Airport Friedrichshafen (Lake Constance airport)* with its runway, on the right you can see the fairground of *Friedrichshafen.*

Langenargen – Im Jahre 770 erstmals als Argona erwähnt, ab 1920 im Besitz der Grafen von Montfort.
Langenargen – the first records of the town date back 770, since 1920 it has belonged to the *Count of Montfort.*

Langenargen am Bodensee und das Schloss Montfort – geprägt durch die geschichtliche Verbindung zu den Grafen von Montfort.
Langenargen, Lake Constance and its *Montfort Castle* - influenced by its historical connections to the *Count of Montfort.*

Eine Luftschiffreise mit Blick auf die verschneite Bodenseelandschaft führt uns über Kressbronn, die südöstlichste Gemeinde des Bundeslandes Baden-Württemberg

A trip on an airship looking down on a snow-covered *Lake Constance* takes us over *Kressbronn*, the most south-eastern municipality of the German state *Baden-Württemberg*.

Nonnenhorn, idyllisches Weindorf am „Bayerischen Bodensee".
Nonnenhorn, an idyllic winemaking village on the shores of the "*Bavarian Lake Constance*".

Die Ortschaft Wasserburg, eine Perle am bayerischen Bodenseeufer zwischen Nonnenhorn und Lindau.
The municipality of *Wasserburg*, a real gem on the Bavarian shores of *Lake Constance* between *Nonnenhorn* and *Lindau*.

Bayern von einer seiner schönsten Seiten: Die Insel Lindau im Bodensee.
Bavaria at its most beautiful: The island of *Lindau* on *Lake Constance.*

Traumhafte, historische Gebäudeensembles auf der Insel Lindau, im Vordergrund der Yachthafen.
Beautiful historical buildings on the island of *Lindau* with the Yachting harbour in the foreground.

Blick über die Insel Lindau zum Rheindamm und zu der Mündung des „Neuen Rheins". Weit öffnet sich das Rheintal und ebnet den Weg zu den Alpen.
Views over the island of *Lindau* to the *River Rhine dam* and the mouth of the *New Rhine*. The *Rheintal* opens right up revealing the way into the alps.

Vor der herrlichen Alpenkulisse mit dem Pfänder überquert ein Luftschiff die Bregenzer Bucht.
An airship crosses *Bregenz* bay in front of breathtaking Alpine background dominated by the *Pfänder* mountain.

Generalblick über den Bodensee von Ost nach West in der beeindruckenden Stimmung eines Sonnenuntergangs. Wozu noch viele Worte verlieren...?
A general view across *Lake Constance* from east to west accompanied by the impressive atmosphere of sunset. Enough said!

Blick auf die Vorarlberger Landeshauptstadt Bregenz (Österreich) mit der Bregenzer Aach.
An overview of *Bregenz*, the provincial capital of *Vorarlberg (Austria)*, including the *Bregenzer Aach* river.

Die Vorarlberger Landeshauptstadt Bregenz mit dem Hausberg Pfänder und der weltberühmten Seebühne.
Bregenz is the provincial capital of *Vorarlberg* and is pictured with its home *Pfänder* mountain and the worldfamous lake stage.

Blick ins Rheintal mit dem „Alten Rhein" und dem Flughafen St. Gallen/Altenrhein im Vordergrund. Die herrliche Kulisse läßt erahnen, was Piloten empfinden.

Views down the *Rheintal* with the *Old Rhine* in front and the airport *St. Gallen/Altenrhein*. The breathtaking Alpine background provides an insight into the wonderful sights that welcome pilots.

Unterhalb des Rorschacher Berges liegt die Schweizer Stadt Rorschach. Der idyllische Hafen und die Promenade laden ein zum Verweilen.
Below the *Rorschacher* mountain lies the Swiss town of *Rorschach*. The idyllic harbour and the promenade provide a lovely place for while away.

Unser Flug führt vorbei an St. Gallen (Schweiz). Herzstück der markanten Altstadt ist das ehemalige Kloster. Es beherbergt die Kantonalregierung. Tagungsort des Kantonalrates ist der einstige barocke Thronsaal des Fürstabtes.

Our route takes us past *St. Gallen (Switzerland)*. The former monastery is at the heart of its old town. It now accommodates the canton government. The council meets up in the former baroque throne room of the Prince Abbot.

Mit Vollgas und im Steigflug nehmen wir Kurs in Richtung Süden und steigen auf eine Höhe von 2470 Meter über NN, um den Gipfel des Säntis zu erreichen. Der Säntis gilt als „Hausberg“ des Bodensees.

Climbing at full power we head south rising to an altitude of 2470 meters above sealevel in order to reach the peak of the *Säntis* mountain. The *Säntis* is regarded as the *„Mountain of Lake Constance“*.

Nach diesem Ausflug ins Landesinnere sinken wir wieder im Gleitflug auf eine Höhe von cirka 600 Meter über den Meeresspiegel und erreichen westlich von Rorschach die Schweizer Ortschaft Horn.

After the excursion inland, we start gliding down again to an altitude of approximately 600 meters above sea level before reaching the Swiss community of *Horn* to the west of *Rorschach*.

Wir genießen wieder die Nähe zum Bodensee in vollen Zügen und gleiten entlang des Ufers in westlicher Richtung, vorbei an der Gemeinde Steinach.

Once again it's a real joy to be close to *Lake Constance* as we glide along the shoreline westwards passing the community of *Steinach*.

Unser nächstes Ziel ist die Schweizer Stadt Arbon, von wo aus wir einen Blick zum Säntis im Hintergrund werfen.
Our next target is the Swiss town of *Arbon* with views to the *Säntis* mountain in the background.

Die Schweizer Stadt Romanshorn ist durch die Autofährverbindung mit der deutschen Stadt Friedrichshafen ein wichtiges Bindeglied zum nördlichen Nachbarn.

The Swiss town of *Romanshorn* has become an important link to its northern neighbour thanks to the car-ferry connections to the German town of *Friedrichshafen*.

Immer weiter führt uns der Flug nach Westen, vorbei an Güttingen (Schweiz) und der herrlichen Alpenkulisse.
Our flight continues to take us further westwards, passing *Güttingen (Switzerland)* against the gorgeous alpine backdrop.

Nach wenigen Minuten Flug erreichen wir die Schweizer Ortschaften Landschlacht und Seedorf, werfen einen Blick zurück und erkennen im Hintergrung gerade noch Altnau.
After flying for just a few minutes we arrive at the Swiss communities of *Landschlacht* and *Seedorf*, looking back we can just about still make out the community of *Altnau*.

Unser nächstes Ziel ist Münsterlingen, wo wir als markantestes Bauwerk die Klosterkirche erblicken. Sicher ist dieses herausragende Bauwerk eine Besichtigung wert.

Out next destination is *Münsterlingen*, where we are greeted by the prominent convent church building. This marvellous building is well worth a visit.

Unsere Flugroute führt uns vorbei an der Schweizer Gemeinde Bottighofen. Die Gegend um Bottighofen war schon in prähistorischer Zeit besiedelt, wie Reste von Seeufersiedlungen zeigen.
Our planned flight takes us past the Swiss municipality of *Bottighofen*. Remains of shore-side settlements provide evidence that area around *Bottighofen* was populated during pre-historic times.

Zwei Städte, die wirken wie eine: Im Vordergrund sehen wir die Schweizer Stadt Kreuzlingen, dahinter Konstanz und die Konstanzer Bucht. „Grenzenlos" ist der herrliche Ausblick über die verschneite Landschaft.

Two towns that look like one: In the foreground we can see the swiss town of *Kreuzlingen*, while behind is *Constance* with *Constance bay*. The breathtaking panorama over the snow-covered landscape is "boundless".

Die Stadt Kreuzlingen, welche direkt an Konstanz angrenzt, ist die größte Schweizer Stadt am Bodensee und bezeichnet sich gern selbst als „die erste Stadt der Schweiz".

The town of *Kreuzlingen* is located directly next to *Constance* and is the largest Swiss town at *Lake Constance*; it likes to refer to itself as „the first town of *Switzerland*".

Tägerwilen gehört zum Bezirk Kreuzlingen (Kanton Thurgau) und grenzt an den Seerhein, welcher den Obersee mit dem Untersee verbindet.

Tägerwilen belongs to the municipality of *Kreuzlingen* (canton of *Thurgau*) and is right next to the *Seerhein*, which links the upper lake to the lower lake.

Am Untersee liegt die Schweizer Ortschaft Ermatingen. Die Hügel oberhalb Ermatingen erlauben einen Blick über die Insel Reichenau, den Bodanrück und das Wollmatinger Ried bis nach Konstanz.

The Swiss municipality of *Ermatingen* is located at the *Untersee* (lower lake). The hills above *Ermatingen* provide views over the island of *Reichenau*, the *Bodanrück*, the *Wollmatinger Ried* and across to *Constance*.

Am Schweizer Bodenseeufer (Untersee) liegt die Ortschaft Berlingen; Ballonfahrer genießen den Anblick aus erhabener Position.
The community of *Berlingen* is located at the Swiss shores of *Lake Constance*. Balloonpilots passing by enjoying this wonderfull view.

Wir passieren die Schweizer Stadt Stadt Steckborn. Am Ufer dominiert das architektonisch beeindruckende Gebäude mit seinen fünf Türmen, dessen Erbauung in das Jahr 1280 zurückreicht. Heute beherbergt das Gebäude das Heimatmuseum.

Passing by the Swiss town of *Steckborn*. Its shores are dominated by the impressive architecture of the building with five towers, which dates back to 1280. Today, the building houses the local museum.

Ein sehenswertes Fleckchen Erde am „Auslauf" des Bodensees – die Schweizer Kleinstadt Stein am Rhein mit der Klosterinsel Werd .
Here's a small piece of earth that's really worth seeing right on the „outlet" of *Lake Constance* – the small Swiss town of *Stein am Rhein*. In the front you can see the island *Werd* with its convent.

Kann eine Altstadt überhaupt noch schöner sein? Das Schweizer Städtchen Stein am Rhein, umgeben von idyllischen Weinbergen.
It is hard to imagine a more beautiful old town! The Swiss town of *Stein am Rhein*, surrounded by idyllic vineyards.

Zwischen Schaffhausen und Stein am Rhein liegt das malerische Städtchen Diessenhofen (Schweiz). Baudenkmäler von nationaler Bedeutung sind die Altstadt mit Siegelturm, Stadtkirche, Unterhof und die gedeckte Holzbrücke über den Rhein.
The picturesque town of *Diessenhofen (Switzerland)* is located between *Schaffhausen* and *Stein am Rhein*. The old town with its Sealtower, the church, the so-called *Unterhof* and not at least the covered wooden bridge over the *Rhine* are all classified as historical monuments.

Westlich von Diessenhofen liegt das am Rhein gelegene Kloster St.Katharinental, welches Mitte des 13. Jahrhunderts entstanden ist und im Laufe des 19. Jahrhunderts als Kloster aufgelöst wurde.

The monastery of *St.Katharinental* is located at the *Rhine* to the west of *Diessenhofen*. Build during the mid 13th century, the building ceased serving as a monastery during the 19th century.

Der Rheinfall: Über eine Breite von 150 m und einer Höhe von 23 m stürzen bei mittlerer Wasserführung des Rheins etwa 700 Kubikmeter Wasser pro Sekunde über die Felsen.

Rhine falls: Across a width of 150 metres and a height of 23 metres, 700 cubic meters of water per second crash down when the *Rhine* river is at an average level.

Unsere Flugroute führt uns vorbei an Schloss Laufen direkt am Rheinfall. Das Schloss wurde im Jahre 858 erstmals geschichtlich erwähnt. Es war der Stammsitz der Freiherren von Laufen.

Our route takes us past *Laufen* castle right next to the *Rhine* falls. The first references to the castle can be found in the year 858. It was the ancestral seat of the *Baron von Laufen.*

Der Rheinfall bei Schaffhausen/Neuhausen (Schweiz) ist der größte Wasserfall Europas. Er bietet dem Besucher ein grandioses Schauspiel.
The *Rheinfall* near *Schaffhausen/Neuhausen (Switzerland)* is Europe`s largest waterfall. Visitors are treated to a magnificent spectacle.

Die eindrucksvolle Stadtfestung Munot ist das Wahrzeichen der Schweizer Stadt Schaffhausen. Die Festung wurde im Zeitraum von 1564 bis 1589 durch Bürger von Schaffhausen in Fronarbeit erbaut.

The impressive *Munot* fortress is the landmark most often associated with the Swiss town of *Schaffhausen*. The fortress was built by the citizens of *Schaffhausen* between 1564 and 1589, working under conditions of enforced labour.

Auf unserem Rückflug passieren wir kurz hinter der Schweizer Grenze die Höriortschaft Öhningen (Deutschland). Nördlich von Öhningen erhebt sich der Schienerberg auf eine Höhe von 703 m über den Meeresspiegel.
On our flight back straight behind the border of *Switzerland* and *Germany*, we pass *Öhningen (Germany)*. To the north of *Öhningen*, the *Schiener* mountain rises to a height of 703 m above sea level.

Ein nach Süd-Ost ausgerichteter Hang bietet der Ortschaft Wangen auf der Halbinsel Höri eine herrliche Wohnlage mit einem weiten Blick in die benachbarte Schweiz.

A south-east-facing slope provides the community of *Wangen* on the *Höri* peninsula a wonderful location with extensive view across into neighbouring *Switzerland.*

Wir fliegen vorbei an der Ortschaft Hemmenhofen auf der Halbinsel Höri. Hemmenhofen war bevorzugtes Domizil berühmter Künstler wie zum Beispiel Otto Dix. Spuren seines Lebens und Wirkens finden wir in seinem Wohnhaus in Hemmenhofen, welches er 1936 bezog.
We pass the community of *Hemmenhofen*, located on the *Höri* peninsula. *Hemmenhofen* has been a favourite location for famous artists such as *Otto Dix*. Traces of his life and impact can be discovered in his house in *Hemmenhofen*, which he moved into in 1936.

Der Flug führt uns vorbei an der Ortschaft Gaienhofen. Direkt am See liegt das Internatsgymnasium und bietet Schülern aus allen Teilen Deutschlands ein traumhaftes Domizil zum Lernen und für die Freizeit. Sport, speziell in Verbindung mit dem See, ist besonders angesagt.
Our flight takes us past the community of *Gaienhofen*. The boarding school is located right next to the lake and offers pupils from across Germany a wonderful place in which to study and to enjoy their leisure time. Sports, especially those associated with the lake, are particularly popular.

Sie erinnern sich noch? Der Flug führte uns heute vorbei an der Schweizer Ortschaft Horn. Vor uns liegt der deutsche „Namensvetter", die Ortschaft Horn. Sie liegt in exponierter Lage an der Spitze der Halbinsel Höri und bietet eine Traumsicht auf die Insel Reichenau.
Time to cast your mind back! Our flight today took us past the Swiss municipality of *Horn*. In front of us is the German municipality that shares the same name. It is located in an exposed position at the tip of the peninsula and offers wonderful views of the island of *Reichenau* and across the lower lake.

Gesamtansicht der „Künstler-Halbinsel" Höri, im Hintergrund der schneebedeckte Feldberg und die Vogesen.
The „artists' peninsula" of *Höri* as general view, in the background you can see the snow-covered *Feldberg* and *Vogesen* mountains.

Kurz bevor wir den Ausgangspunkt unserer „Bilderreise" wieder erreichen, werfen wir noch einen Blick auf drei Ortschaften der vorderen Höri: Vorn im Bild erkennen wir Iznang, links dahinter Weiler und rechts Bankholzen, flankiert von der Nordseite des Schienerberges.
Just before returning to the starting point of our "pictorial journey", we get another opportunity to take in the views of *Höri* with its three municipalities: In the foreground is *Iznang*, behind it and to the left *Weiler*, and *Bankholzen* to the right, flanked by the north face of the *Schiener* mountain.

Nun befinden wir uns südlich der Ortschaft Moos und blicken über den „Zeller See", wo wir Radolfzell und die Halbinsel Mettnau erkennen. Ein traumhafter Flug geht dem Ende zu, nicht jedoch, ohne Ihnen auf der folgenden Seite noch ein Highlight zu präsentieren...

Now we find ourselves to the south of *Moos* looking over what is known locally as the "*Zeller See*", where we can make out *Radolfzell* and the *Mettnau* peninsula. A wonderful flight is coming to an end, but not before presenting you with one more highlight on the centre spread that follows...

Mit dieser Gesamtansicht des Bodensees danke ich Ihnen, dass Sie mit mir diese Bilderreise unternommen haben. Ich freue mich heute schon darauf, bei einem meiner nächsten Projekte wieder „Ihr Pilot“ sein zu dürfen. Herzliche Grüße aus Radolfzell am Bodensee, Ihr Stanko Petek.

I would like to use this overall shot of *Lake Constance* to say thank you for accompanying me on this "pictorial journey". I hope that you have enjoyed it and that you will be on board again for one of my next projects. Wishing you all the best from *Radolfzell*, yours *Stanko Petek*.

Fliegen mit Seeblick

Der Bodensee-Airport ist einer der ältesten Flugplätze der Welt. Schon die Zeppeline des Luftschiffpioniers Ferdinand Graf von Zeppelin erhoben sich von hier aus. Aufgrund der in den letzten Jahren erfolgten Investitionen wird der Bodensee-Airport Friedrichshafen heute von großen Passagierflugzeugen angeflogen, z. B. A 320. Möglich macht dies die 2.354 m lange Start- und Landebahn sowie die technischen Einrichtungen von internationalem Standard. Selbst bei starken Nebellagen am Bodensee-Airport Friedrichshafen ist es möglich sicher zu starten und zu landen. Im Jahr 2005 nutzten nahezu 600.000 Fluggäste den Bodensee-Airport Friedrichshafen. Die Fluggäste aus Süd-Deutschland, Vorarlberg (Österreich), dem Fürstentum Liechtenstein und der Ostschweiz bevorzugen den Regionalflughafen auf Grund seiner großen Vielfalt an direkten Flugzielen.
Die Betreibergesellschaft hat es sich zur Aufgabe gemacht, den Umweltschutz bei den Unternehmensplanungen besonders zu berücksichtigen und Eingriffe in die Umwelt und Natur entsprechend dem Stand der Technik zu minimieren. Im Jahr 2003 schaffte es der Bodensee-Airport Friedrichshafen als erster Regionalflughafen in Deutschland nach EMAS validiert zu werden. Eine weitere Validierung wurde 2006 durchgeführt und mit Bravur bestanden. Für alle Flugbegeisterten gibt es noch zwei besondere Attraktionen am Bodensee-Airport Friedrichshafen: die kostenlose Besucherterrasse und ein Panorama Restaurant mit Blick auf die Start- und Landebahn, den Hangar des Zeppelin NT sowie die Neue Messe Friedrichshafen.

Das Team des Bodensee-Airport Friedrichshafen würde sich freuen, auch Sie schon bald begrüßen zu dürfen, sei es als Fluggast oder einfach nur, um am Bodensee-Airport die Faszination des Fliegens hautnah zu erleben.

Bodensee-Airport Friedrichshafen
Postfach 1520, D-88005 Friedrichshafen
Tel.: +49 (7541) 284-01
Fax: +49 (7541) 284-207
e-mail: info@fly-away.de
http://www.fly-away.de

Bodensee-Airport
FRIEDRICHSHAFEN

Impressum

Telefon: +49 (0) 7732-141400 · Telefax: +49 (0) 7732-141404
email: info@luftbild.com · internetportal: www.Luftbild.com

Konzeption: Stanko Petek
Conception: Stanko Petek
Texte: Stanko Petek
Text: Stanko Petek
Übersetzung: twiggs translation
Translation: twiggs translation
Gestaltung: Stanko Petek
Design: Stanko Petek
Photos: Stanko Petek · www.luftbild.com
Photos: Stanko Petek · www.luftbild.com
Herstellung: Druck Schefenacker · www.schefenacker-druck.de
Production: Druck Schefenacker · www.schefenacker-druck.de

5. Auflage : 6.000 Exemplare
5th edition : 6.000 copies

ISBN: 978-3-93789-313-6